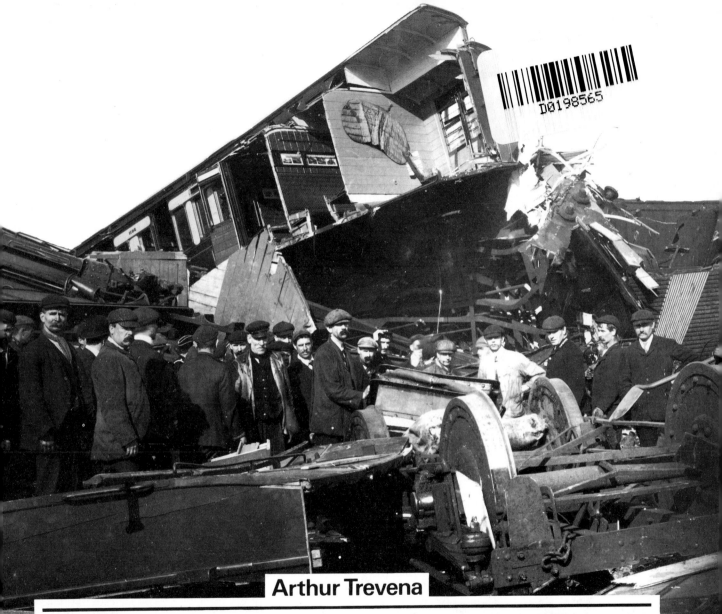

Arthur Trevena

# TRAINS in TROUBLE
## VOLUME TWO
### RAILWAY ACCIDENTS IN PICTURES

# Introduction

This is the second in a projected four-part series, under the 'Trains in Trouble' title, which deals pictorially with accidents on British railways — with one or two examples from abroad — over a period of some 120 years. The intention is not to dwell on tragedy: casualty figures are included only in so far as they inevitably reflect the seriousness of an incident, and the author makes no apology for including accidents in which no fatalities occurred. Rather, the intention has been to portray a representative cross-section of types of accident.

In the continuing quest for a safer railway, the company engineers' twin preoccupations were, firstly, the perfection of mechanical and operational safeguards to offset human fallibility and, secondly, in recognition of the fact that the number of accidents might be thus reduced but never entirely eliminated, the development of coaching stock construction to minimise their effects. That the latter endeavour has met with considerable success can be seen by comparing the photographs taken at Wellingborough in 1898 and at Prestonpans in 1980. In both cases, speeding expresses hit obstructions on the track.

Upon reading this book, the reader may well reflect on the truth of the old maxim that accidents do not just happen, they are *caused*. In the case of the railway accident, the cause can nearly always be traced back to some error on the part of railwaymen who, in a moment of weakness such as we all experience, set in motion an irreversible series of events which ended in tragedy — often before their very eyes. Of the 49 incidents included in this book, 32 were caused directly by human error, and in almost all the other cases it was a major contributory factor.

But if the elements of disaster can reveal the weaknesses of the human spirit, they can also summon its finest attributes. Featured in this book is the ammunition train explosion at Soham in 1944 — one of the most spectacular railway accidents ever to occur in Britain — after which both enginemen were awarded the George Cross in recognition of courage of the highest order. This was the first instance in Britain in WWII of an explosion on a moving train — a fact which reflects tremendous credit on the wartime operation of British railways. It also, incidentally, demonstrated the great robustness of the steam locomotive, for 2-8-0 No.7337 was repaired and survived until 1967 as Longmoor Military Railway No.400 *Sir Guy Williams*.

Great Western enthusiasts, who will be disappointed (or gratified, as the case may be) to find that company under-represented in these pages, may well be aware that this is evidence of its enviable safety record. The featured accidents at Slough and Llanelly were the only major disasters to tarnish that record between 1890 (Norton Fitzwarren) and 1936 (Shrivenham) — both featured in 'Trains in Trouble Vol.I'. The GWR's Automatic Train Control system, which provided audible cab warning of a distant signal at danger, was largely responsible for this happy state of affairs — a fact continually and unsuccessfully drawn to the attention of other railway companies by the Railway Inspectorate.

Research for the captions has revealed many curiosities — the fact, for example, that certain locations attract disaster (Goswick, Penistone, Norton Fitzwarren, etc); or semi-comic incidents — such as the hundreds of Christmas puddings which littered the track after the derailment at Aylesbury, and which were largely cleared by the inhabitants of that town. A singularly poignant fact to come to light was that the express driver killed in the 1913 Colchester collision, one William Henry Barnard of Ipswich, was the son of John Barnard — himself killed when the boiler of 0-6-0 No.522 exploded at Westerfield in 1900, an incident illustrated in Volume I of this series.

The details for most of the captions which follow were taken from the official reports of the Railway Inspectorate: that worthy body empowered by Parliamentary Acts of 1840 and 1842 to investigate the causes of British railway accidents. These meticulously detailed documents, open to inspection at the Public Records Office, make fascinating if sobering reading, and might well instil in today's rail traveller a sense of gratitude that the railway accident has always been treated as the matter of the utmost gravity and concern. Other details were taken from LTC Rolt's classic 'Red for Danger' (Bodley Head, David & Charles, Pan Books) and from OS Nock's 'Historic Railway Disasters' (Ian Allan, Arrow Books), both of which are recommended further reading.

Finally, the reader is reminded that the photographs which follow depict incidents notable for their rarity, and that his own home is a far more hazardous environment than a British railway carriage.

---

*Front cover*: The locomotives of a doubleheaded goods — 0-6-0's Nos.1219 and 1135 — derailed at Winston, NER, on 24th October 1905. Platelayers had removed a rail. *Photo: K. Hoole collection*
*Back cover*: D1072 *Western Glory* being jacked upright during a rerailing exercise at Bristol Bath Road on 12th January 1977. *Photo: T.W. Nicholls*
*Title page*: The wreckage of the Night Mail at Shrewsbury on October 15th 1907. Full details in 'Trains in Trouble Vol.I'
*Photo: Author's collection*
*Opposite*: North Eastern 0-6-0 No.1448 derailed at Lumpsey, c.1930.
*Photo: K. Hoole collection*

## THE AUTHOR

The publishers regret to record, as this book passed to them for publication, the sudden death of Arthur Trevena. The author of five books, including Volume I of 'Trains in Trouble' and many articles on historical subjects, he was also a skilled modelmaker and acknowledged expert on Cornish mining. A fine man, who could communicate informed enthusiasm on many subjects, he will be greatly missed.

## ACKNOWLEDGEMENTS

The author and publishers acknowledge with thanks the assistance given by those who provided material for inclusion in this book: particularly The Railway Inspectorate of the Department of Transport; Ken Hoole; P. N. Townend; C. P. Boocock; H. C. Casserley and Allan Stanistreet.

First published 1981   © Atlantic Books 1981
ISBN 0 906899 03 6      Designed by Nigel Trevena
Printed by Penwell Ltd, Callington, Cornwall

**Published by ATLANTIC BOOKS**
**25 Scorrier Street   St Day   Redruth**
**Cornwall TR16 5LH   (0209) 821016**

# TROUBLE WITH BOILERS

It took time for railwaymen responsible for our early railways fully to appreciate the great potential for destruction of the locomotive and its train, and with mechanical contrivances in their infancy and methods of operation generally cavalier and sometimes foolhardy, it is surprising that a far greater number of serious accidents did not occur.

The fact that the locomotive boiler could be a highly destructive device, for example, took some time to be reflected in design and operational practice, and the first three decades of British railway history were punctuated by a series of alarming explosions.

At Wolverton in 1850, for example, a noise-sensitive labourer screwed down a stationary locomotive's safety valves to silence it and, in the ensuing violent explosion, had one of his ears blown off. Near Rugby in 1861, the engine of the Irish Mail completely disintegrated due to a badly corroded boiler barrel; and at Colne in 1864 some parts of a goods engine were blown a quarter of a mile, and others never found at all, in a similar incident.

By 1870 more frequent inspections, improved boilermaking techniques, better quality materials and more stringent regulations all contributed to a steady decline in the number of boiler explosions. However, enginemen had long been accustomed to tamper with the safety valves of their locomotives in the search for more power, and the habit died hard. The incident shown here took place at Lewes, LBSCR, on 27th September 1879. 2-4-0 No.174, hauling a Hastings-London passenger train carrying the local MP, had stopped at the station and took water while the driver went round with his oil can. As Driver Rookwood received the 'right-away' and eased forward, the firebox blew up, showering the train and station with steam, boiling water, soot, coal and ballast. The engine was thrown off the rails, its smokebox door blown off, and Rookwood was found dead on the roof of the second carriage. His fireman and guard were injured but survived.

Subsequent examination by Stroudley and his staff revealed that No.174's safety valves had been tampered with and set to blow off at 140 psi instead of 120. The explosion had occurred at the former pressure.

*Photo: Author's collection*

# THE RUNAWAY TRAIN

The appalling series of events which took place on the Irish Great Northern Railway's Newry-Armagh branch on 12th June 1889 have been chronicled in print before. However, since their significance is indisputable — Rolt defined the disaster as 'possibly the most significant of all' — the story is repeated here with what is believed to be an unpublished photograph.

Armagh terminus was situated at the foot of a three mile gradient of between 1 in 75 and 1 in 82; the single line was worked by staff and ticket and trains were despatched at intervals of 10 or 20 minutes. On that particular summer's day, a fifteen vehicle train, packed with 940 passengers, was booked to leave Armagh hauled by a four-coupled tender engine. The driver, Thomas McGrath, complained to the stationmaster that this locomotive was inadequate for the job and requested a larger engine. His request was turned down and he himself, in ill temper, rejected the offer of a banker to the summit.

In fact, McGrath's engine should, in theory, have managed the train on the bank but, within sight of the summit, it stalled. There then began a sequence of events which, had their result not been so appalling, could be seen to contain all the elements of high comedy.

McGrath and James Eliot, the latter the Company official in charge of the excursion, knew that a second train from Armagh was due shortly, and that this could assist them over the summit. This solution they rejected. They resolved to divide their train, taking part forward to the next station and returning for the rest. Eliot accordingly instructed the front acting guard, William Moorhead, to uncouple between the fifth and sixth carriages. The braking system in use, as all the men in charge of the train knew, was of a simple, primitive pattern which ceased to function when air was admitted — the opposite to modern practice and, in the circumstances, a potentially lethal device.

With only the hand brake in the rear guards van and a few stones placed behind their wheels to hold them on the gradient, the last ten carriages were uncoupled. To enable Moorhead to lift the hook, McGrath eased his engine back to slacken the coupling, and as he did so he nudged the buffers of the leading carriage. It was just enough to start the uncoupled train rolling slowly backwards, crushing the stones to powder. In the brake van, desperate attempts were made to screw down the handbrake, while McGrath set back further as Moorhead frantically tried to re-couple. Twice he almost succeeded and twice he tripped and dropped the coupling. Stones were pushed under the now rapidly revolving wheels, but to no avail. None of the passengers in the runaway coaches could help. In accordance with Company regulations all the doors had been locked at Armagh, and as the runaway train accelerated down the bank not a soul could escape.

Meanwhile, the next train had left Armagh and, with only six vehicles, was steaming hard up the gradient. About 1½ miles from the summit the fireman saw the runaway carriages swaying down the line towards him. They had run for 1¼ miles, gathering speed all the time.

In the terrible impact the locomotive fell on its side and against it the wooden carriages of the excursion shattered themselves to pieces and were hurled down the 40 foot embankment. The second train broke into two halves and these too began to roll backwards, only being brought to a stand by prompt action by the shocked and injured driver and guard.

Eighty people, including many children, died at Armagh and as many more were seriously injured. It was the worst railway accident to date and, in terms of fatalities, has rarely been surpassed. There was considerable reaction from a shocked public, and in many ways the disaster marked the end of the primitive methods and technology of the early railways and helped to seal their fate. Within a few months, two fundamentals of safe railway working — the continuous automatic brake and absolute block working — were made law. The railway companies were forced into a new era of operation and the eighty victims of Armagh had not died in vain.

*Photo: Author's collection*

## THE WORST NATURAL ENEMY

While not depicting a railway accident as such, this remarkable picture is surely an outstanding portrait of a 'train in trouble'. The location was County March Summit, just south of Altnabreac on the Highland Railway; almost as far north as it is possible to get on Britain's railway system and 708 feet above sea level. The locomotive, a snowplough-equipped Jones 4-4-0 leading two similar engines, was about to do battle with drifts which were forty feet deep in places. The date was 8th March 1895.

*Photo: Author's collection*

# SAFETY MARGINS CUT?

During the summer of 1895, the fierce rivalry between the Great Northern, North Eastern and North British on the east coast, and the London & North Western on the west coast, led to higher and higher speeds on the competing routes into Scotland. In the interests of cutting seconds off already tight schedules, crews and locomotives were pushed to the limit, and at certain places on the routes the margin of safety was cut to the barest minimum.

These races to the north left a legacy of tight schedules, and in the following year the high speed derailment at Preston on 15th August was seen by many as the inevitable result of unwarranted competition and caused a great public outcry.

The Scottish tourist sleeping car express, leaving Euston at 8 pm, was allowed just 112 minutes to cover the 105 miles from Wigan to Carlisle, a schedule which demanded footplate work of the highest order. On the night in question, however, neither driver of the doubleheaded express had worked the train before, and neither had worked non-stop through the awkward curves at Preston, where there was a speed restriction of 10 mph.

When the 200 ton train passed through the station at 45 mph, the results were spectacular. At the sharp curve just north of the platforms the engines — Webb 2-4-0's No.2159 *Shark* and No.275 *Vulcan* — leapt the rails and ploughed straight on into the ballast. Both remained upright but the carriages were hurled in all directions, only their robust modern construction keeping the casualties mercifully low — only one fatality occurring.

*Photo: Author's collection*

# STIRLING SINGLE IN TROUBLE

On 7th March 1896 the 5.30 up Great Northern express, Leeds to King's Cross, was running at speed through Little Bytham, just south of Stoke summit, when the last of the eight carriages became derailed. Most of the others subsequently left the track; the seventh and eighth running down the embankment, and two passengers in the sixth were killed.

A PW gang had recently relaid the track at the point of derailment and had prematurely removed the speed restriction signs. This was compounded by the abnormally heavy axle loading of the express engine - Stirling Single No.1003 — and the accident contributed to the decision to rebuild the six engines of the class with a reduced axle loading.

*Photo: Author's collection*

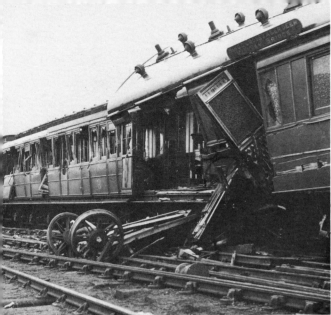

DUNBAR 1898

## EXPRESS RAMS GOODS

On 3rd January 1898, at Dunbar on the North British main line north of Berwick, the wagons of a goods train were being shunted across the down line into the goods yard when several became derailed. Although the section was protected by a home signal at danger, the driver of an approaching King's Cross-Aberdeen express failed to observe it, and his locomotive hit the rear of the goods engine, throwing it on to its side. Some telescoping of carriages occurred, one person was killed and 21 hurt.

*Photos: Author's collection*

ST JOHNS 1898

## FATAL ERROR BY SIGNALMAN     *(Right)*

A similar incident occurred some two months later, on 21st March, at St Johns, SECR. The up 7 am Hastings Parlour Car Express headed by the pioneer Stirling F Class 4-4-0 No.205 ran into the rear of the 7.45 am Tonbridge-Charing Cross passenger, which was standing in fog at the up home signal. Again, telescoping took place, killing three and injuring twenty. The cause lay in a mistake by the signalman, who believed that the Tonbridge train had left his section and cleared the path for that from Hastings.

*Photo: Author's collection*

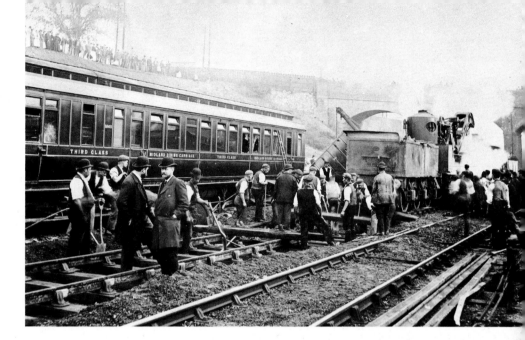

## THE RUNAWAY TROLLEY

At Wellingborough station on the Midland main line, on 2nd September 1898, a postman pushing a luggage trolley left it momentarily unattended while he opened a gate through which to take it. Although he turned the handle to apply its front wheel lock, the trolley rolled forward down the slight gradient (8'' in 16'), tipped over the platform edge and fell across the down fast line. The 7.15 St Pancras to Manchester dining car express was due to pass and two railwaymen made heroic attempts to clear the obstruction, but had to jump for their lives as the express entered the station at a mile a minute. 4-4-0 No.1743 (later No.363) hit the trolley, was partially derailed and, at the diamond crossover at the northern end of the station, was hurled onto its side.

Damage to the leading coaches was severe, the second being completely wrecked, and seven people were killed and 65 injured. Few major railway accidents have had so simple a cause and in the subsequent enquiry the Midland Railway was reminded that the design and operation of every part of the railway were subjects for continuing concern and vigilance.

*All photos: Author's collection*

The aftermath of the disaster
at Wellingborough.
*Left*: There were plenty of volun-
teers to help clear the wreckage.
*Below*: The hulk of the loco
motive involved: 4-4-0 No.1743.
*Right*: The remains of the second
coach — a 12-wheeler.

*All photos: Author's collection*

## PENMAENMAWR 1899

# ENGINEMEN DROWNED

Storm and tempest, and their resultant floods and landslips, can cause operational problems but only rarely have they been the direct causes of railway accidents. A most unusual incident occurred on the night of 12th January 1899 in North Wales, where the LNWR line hugged the coast.

A combination of high tides and storm force winds meant that a close watch was being kept on the state of the permanent way on that vulnerable stretch of track. During the height of the storm, waves breached the retaining wall near Penmaenmawr and washed away a substantial amount of ballast, leaving several hundred yards of track unsupported. Two platelayers witnessed the occurrence and ran, in opposite directions, to warn approaching traffic.

The unfortunate man heading in the Chester direction was hurrying through a tunnel some 150 yards from the breach when an express goods entered in front of him. He had no way of knowing if his warning signal was seen by the crew of Class DX No.1418 but, in any event, it was too late to stop the train. In the violent derailment the locomotive wrenched the track almost to right angles and tossed its crew into the sea where they both drowned.

*Photos: Author's collection*

## CALEDONIAN COLLISION

On 23rd October 1899, the 6.55 pm express ex-Perth was passing Coupar Angus station on the Caledonian Railway when it was in violent sidelong collision with a cattle train emerging from a siding. The express engine — CR 4-4-0 No.13 — was damaged and, as the picture shows, the goods engine was almost completely demolished. This was 2-4-0 No.431 and it was subsequently scrapped; Driver Pyper of Aberdeen was killed on his footplate.

*Photos: Author's collection*

# DISASTER ON RACE DAY

These photographs show the scene at Slough station (GWR) on 16th June 1900 — Windsor Race Day — after 7'8" Single No.3015 *Kennet*, hauling the 1.15 Paddington to Falmouth express, had run into the rear of the late running 1.05 pm Paddington-Windsor train standing at the down main platform.

No.3015's driver missed the signals at Dolphin Junction and the distant for Slough East box, and his fireman had to draw his attention to the home signal at Slough East box, which was at danger to protect the passenger train at the platform.

By then, No.3015, not booked to stop at Slough and which had been fired hard between Langley and Dolphin Junction, was running at some sixty miles an hour. The wretched driver made an emergency brake application, put his engine into reverse and threw open his sand blast valves, but all was in vain.

In the wreckage of the collision five people died and 35 were seriously injured.

Another view of the accident at Slough. Note the composite coach with its central guards compartment, a layout used occasionally in the 1890s, with plush 1st Class seating to be seen at the near end and a more spartan interior further from the camera.

*All photos: Author's collection*

## THE PLIGHT OF NO.1433 *(Right)*

The two following evocative photographs show a derailed lime train at Peckwash on the Midland Derby-Ambergate line on 1st December 1900. The locomotive is MR 0-6-0 No.1433 (later No. 3051) and the demolished rail built buffer stops beneath it suggests a runaway, diverted into a siding to stop its flight.

*Photos: Author's collection*

Another view of
the accident
at Peckwash.

**CARLISLE 1902**

## AN UNHAPPY CHRISTMAS

Denton Holme Goods Yard, G&SWJR, Carlisle on Christmas Eve 1902. The driver of Stirling 0-6-0 No.100A, hauling empty wagons, mistook a siding for a running line and ended up in the adjacent roadway.

*Photo: Author's collection*

## MYSTERY OF THE NIGHT EXPRESS

On 23rd December 1904, the 2.45 am express left Marylebone hauled by GCR Robinson 4-4-0 No.1040. The stock was mixed: three fish vans, a meat van, parcels van and brake as well as coaches carrying GCR employees. Running at high speed through heavy fog, the train approached speed-restricted Aylesbury station (GCR-Metropolitan joint) much too fast. The engine, tender and four coaches mounted the down platform and the rest of the train was scattered for fifty yards along both running lines.

Almost at once, the 10.20 pm ex-Manchester GCR express ran into the wreckage, but its driver had made an emergency brake application and damage to his train was superficial.

The crew of No.1040 was killed, together with two passengers, and the derailment has never been satisfactorily explained. It would seem that the driver missed the 15 mph speed restriction board, which gave only 200 yards warning and was all but invisible on a foggy night. Sam Fay later persuaded the Metropolitan to ease the curves at Aylesbury.

Photos: Author's collection

## LLANELLY 1904

# A RARE GREAT WESTERN DISASTER

The incident at Llanelly is simply described, but was never satisfactorily explained. A Neyland-Paddington corridor express, doubleheaded by 1661 Class 0-6-0ST No.1674 (leading) and Bulldog 4-4-0 No.3460 *Montreal*, and consisting of eight 8-wheeled bogies and a milk tank wagon, left the rails at Loughor Bridge, two miles east of Llanelly. Engines and stock fell down a six-foot embankment and five people were killed, including the crew of the tank engine, and 18 injured.

At the enquiry, the inspector could find no direct evidence of cause — the line was straight and level and no mechanical defect could be detected. However, the surviving driver insisted that his speed had been 25-30 mph, but passing timings gave a different figure — about 60 mph — pointing to excessive speed as the most likely cause of the disaster.

A contributory factor was considered to be the surging of water in the saddle tanks of the pilot engine. The GWR had just introduced the pannier tank design and this derailment confirmed the wisdom of the decision to convert the many 0-6-0 saddle tanks to pannier tanks, which was a lengthy process starting generally in 1909. The 1661 Class was unusual in having frames intended for a further batch of Dean Goods double framed 0-6-0s and their 5ft driving wheels — as against the more usual 4ft7½in — would have enabled them to run at higher speeds for which their braking power was inadequate. They were unpopular engines and eight were sold to minor South Wales railways in 1906, only to return to the GWR fold in 1922. *Photos: Author's collection*

# NEGLIGENCE ON THE GREAT EASTERN?

Witham lay on the GER main London-Colchester line. On the morning of 1st September 1905, three platelayers were working on a trailing crossover at the approach to the station. Although they later strenuously denied it, the accident inspector concluded that they had negligently loosened the rail fastenings in the 'V' of the crossing. A second or two later they looked up to see the 9.27 am express to Cromer bearing down on them at 70 miles an hour. The platelayers stepped back, their eyes fixed on a particular spot on the track, and then witnessed the spectacular derailment of the entire fourteen coach train.

The first three coaches broke loose and were thrown beyond the station, one catching fire; the next five fouled the down platform and demolished station buildings, and a ninth was hurled onto its roof and destroyed. Nine people were killed and, in the subsequent enquiry, there was some evidence of a company cover-up of the true causes of the accident.

*Photos: Author's collection*

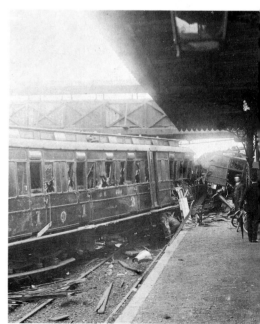

# THE DANGEROUS CROSSOVER : 1

On the night of 28th August 1907, Signalman William Hay was the only railwayman on duty at the North Eastern Railway's station at Goswick, on what is now the East Coast Main Line. His box was sited on the up side at the southern end of the platform and adjacent to a level crossing. Some 260 feet further south lay facing points leading to an up independent line which commenced at that point and ran for two miles to the next station, Beal. It was a simple well signalled layout, with good visibility and a gentle gradient, but was to be the scene of three major accidents: in 1953, 1947 (qv) and, the first, 1907.

The night of the 28th of August of that year was a clear one, and Signalman Hay had no reason to expect that it would be any different to any other in his 13 years as a signalman. At 12.24 am the 11.10 up goods approached Goswick. It was the practice for southbound goods trains to be diverted at Goswick onto the independent line as far as Beal and the company's regulation No.148 stipulated that the crossover be negotiated at 5 mph. Accordingly, Driver Bennett reduced speed almost to a stand at Hay's box and entered the independent line at near walking pace. Four minutes later, the 10.55 Edinburgh-London express roared through Goswick on the clear main line.

Now, the same combination of trains which had just passed Goswick safely: goods and express passenger, was shortly afterwards again approaching the station, but this time things were to go fatally wrong. At 12.28 Hay sent the 'train out of section' signal to the signalman at Scremerston — who controlled the next section north-wards — and was offered another goods, the 11.22. Hay accepted it, but kept all his signals at danger while he offered it onwards to Beal. Beal's Signalman Brown first checked on the whereabouts of the 11.15 Edinburgh-London express. This was reported as just leaving Berwick and, since it would need the up main through Goswick, Brown told Hay to shunt the 11.22 goods onto the independent line, which the previous goods train still occupied at Beal.

So far, so good: the chain of signalmen controlling the main line were going through well-worked procedures devised to ensure the safe passage of trains. The elaborate systems, however, were only safe as long as the locomen observed the signals.

Hay's signals controlling the speed-restricted crossover were all at danger as the goods approached the distant, so he altered the junction points and lowered the intermediate main up signal so that the driver could approach the main up signal where he (Hay) could warn him of the presence of the previous goods train, still held at Beal on the independent line.

The 11.22 Tweedsmouth-Newcastle goods consisted of only 20 vehicles — all vacuum-braked — and the locomotive, 7-year old 4-6-0 No.2005, was making light work of the load. At the regulator was Driver Brown, who had some 18 years' driving experience, but his record was marred by one instance of overrunning a platform, two instances of omitting to stop at scheduled stations, and three instances of overrunning signals. This latter error Brown repeated at Goswick. It was his last mistake.

His train thundered past the main up and up starting signals at danger and, running at express speed, entered the points for the independent line. No.2005 turned completely over and landed in a ditch by the side of the line. Nine wagons were completely destroyed and eight more severely damaged. The guard was badly hurt and Driver Brown and his fireman were killed instantaneously.

*Photo: Author's collection*

# THE ENGINE THAT BROKE ITS BACK

The generally massive construction of the steam locomotive, which made it such a potentially potent instrument of destruction, also meant that it was rare that an engine was destroyed or irreperably damaged in an accident. Indeed, it was not unknown for a locomotive to assist in the recovery of the wrecked stock of its own train. However, the appalling damage suffered by LNWR Ramsbottom Newton 2-4-0 No.1529 *Cook* involved in the high speed derailment at Ditton Junction (LNWR) on 17th September 1912, was an exception to the general rule.

The driver of the 5.30 Chester to Liverpool express, travelling at high speed on the fast line, misread the signals at a point where there were no fewer than eight running lines, and approached a speed-restricted crossover at *four times* the speed he should have done.

The entire train left the rails at 60 mph: the engine, thrown on its side, ploughing up the track until it rammed the pier of an overbridge, demolishing much of the brickwork. The coaches leapt right over the engine and piled in awful confusion beyond the bridge, where gaslighting cylinders burst into flame and turned the mountain of wreckage into an inferno. The enginemen and 13 passengers died.

The picture shows the shocking state of the locomotive. Its back has been broken — the first time this had ever occurred — the boiler barrel having sheared completely from the firebox throat plate.

*Photo: BBC Hulton Picture Library*

# THE COURAGE OF DRIVER FISHER

At 2.11 pm on 12th July 1913, the 1.18 pm train from Harwich arrived at Colchester station on the Great Eastern. The engine, E4 2-4-0 No.471, uncoupled and drew up to the Junction signal box where it took water and was offered to the station box for light engine duties.

The presence of a goods train emerging from the down sidings meant that the 2-4-0 could not be immediately crossed over and, while awaiting instructions, it occupied the up main line. At 2.52, Colchester box offered Junction box the 1 pm up Cromer express and the Junction signalman, in a fatal abberation, forgot the presence of the light engine and accepted the express on the same line. He had not protected the light engine with a collar on his home signal and, using his release key to release the interlocking device, he lowered his starting signal.

On seeing this, the puzzled driver of the light engine, Fisher by name, moved slowly forward and sent his fireman to the signal box to ask the signalman if he knew what he was doing. He then climbed onto his tender and saw to his horror that a train had entered the section behind him. He jumped to the footplate, snapped open the regulator and put on steam but, as his engine picked up speed, the inevitable collision occurred.

The 12-coach Cromer express was running at about 40 mph when it rammed the tender of the light engine in its path, pushing it forward 283 yards and falling on its side across the down main line. The express engine, GER No.1506, was just three months old but was so seriously damaged that only its boiler was salvaged, and the number 1506 remained unfilled thereafter.

The courageous action of Driver Fisher reduced the effects of the collision and, despite considerable damage to stock, only the footplate crew and guard of the express were killed. Fisher himself was amongst the fourteen injured.

*Photos: Author's collection*

## OOH, HECK . . .!

Most stations have their own stories of shunting mishaps, but few have been as spectacular as this at Heck on the North Eastern Selby-Doncaster line in 1923. The carriage knocked the wagons through the buffer stop and, riding on their upturned wheels, mounted the roof of the house.　　*Photo: K. Hoole collection*

## DOWN THE BANK

North Eastern J39 0-6-0 No.1448 — the first of its class and then almost new — derailed at trap points at Lumpsey, near Brotton on the LNER, c.1930. Hundreds of similar minor derailments occurred over the years and did not always warrant a Railway Inspectorate investigation. (See also page 2)　　*Photo: K. Hoole collection*

## RUSH HOUR INCIDENT

Another in a long series of accidents caused by signalmen's errors took place at the height of the morning rush hour on the intensively worked Southern electric suburban lines at Battersea Park on 2nd April 1937. Such a disaster was unexpected, since the Sykes 'lock and block' system, with its complex interlocking of signals, block working and electric treadles activated by passing trains, had resulted in 30 years' safe working of these lines. In a few flustered moments, Signalman Childs, experienced at his job, failed to follow company regulations and over-rode the mechanical system.

The result was a 30 mph rear end collision — the 7.30 am London Bridge-Victoria train was standing at the Battersea Park up local home signal when it was struck by the 7.31 am Coulsdon North-Victoria train. Ten people died and eighty were injured.

*Photo: BBC Hulton Picture Library*

## THREE CRANES NEEDED

Breakdown crews were accustomed to dealing with derailments and other accidents of all kinds and had to be prepared for the worst, but the predicament of WD 2-8-0 No.8247, shown here, must have caused them more problems than most. Three cranes were needed to extricate the locomotive: two 50 ton from Motherwell and Carlisle respectively, and one 20 ton from Polmadie. The location was Wallneuk Junction, Paisley, and the date 21st January 1941. No.8247 was a WD engine on loan to the LMS. With its original number of WD 321, it later went to Persia, returning to the UK in 1948 to be renumbered 48257.

*Photo: Author's collection*

**CREWE 1941**

## LMS BOMBED

Preston-based Stanier Black 5 No.5425 at Crewe Works on 7th April 1941, showing the extensive damage caused in a Luftwaffe air raid. After repair, the engine passed to BR upon nationalisation and, as No.45425, survived until 1967.

*Photo: Author's collection*

# THE DESTRUCTION OF SOHAM

Soham is situated in Cambridgeshire on the Ely-Newmarket Branch of the LNER and was served by a simple country station with passing loop.

The night of 1st-2nd June 1944 was fine and warm, with light variable winds, and the preceding weeks had been exceptionally dry. There was no moon and, of course, no light of any sort to illuminate the passage along the branch of the 11.40 pm Whitemoor-Ipswich freight. In the early hours, WD 2-8-0 No.7337 was making steady progress with 51 open wagons loaded with materials for the many East Anglian air bases engaged in the massive USAAF daylight offensive against enemy occupied Europe. Seven wagons contained components and the rest were packed with 400 tons of 500lb and 250lb bombs.

Proceeding under clear signals at about 20 mph, this monstrous train approached Soham, No.7337 steaming lightly on the level line. A few moments after passing the up distant, Driver Benjamin Gimbert noticed some steam coming from the left hand injector and was watching it from his cab side window when he saw flames coming from the bottom of the leading wagon. There now followed a sequence of events without parallel in British railway history.

Gimbert was well aware of what the wagon contained and, sounding his whistle, brought his train carefully to a stand. Immediately he instructed Fireman Nightall to uncouple the leading wagon, handing him the coal hammer in case the coupling was too hot to touch. Nightall swiftly accomplished this task, but as he remounted the footplate the flames were spreading rapidly.

Meanwhile, the guard had also seen the fire and was hurrying forward to help fight the flames: in his house close to the station, Sub-ganger Fuller had been aroused by shouts for assistance by Signalman Bridges and was watching the drama through his bedroom window as he hurriedly dressed.

With the blazing wagon in tow, Gimbert set forward smartly with the

intention of taking it into open country away from the nearby town, but even in that moment of extreme personal hazard he did not neglect his duty as a railwayman, and slowed to a crawl in the station to tell Signalman Bridges to protect the single line ahead. It was now 1.43 am. As the engine and wagon approached the signal box, the wagon blew up.

In the tremendous detonation, Nightall died instantly and Bridges was mortally injured; Fuller and his family were buried in the rubble of their house, as were the Station-master's family in theirs; and Guard Clarke was knocked flat and stunned. Driver Gimbert, however, had a quite miraculous escape and, although terribly injured, survived on his footplate. No.7337's tender was blown into a twisted mass of steel but the engine itself, although derailed, was only slightly damaged.

The train, safely isolated by Gimbert's action, was almost completely unscathed. Of the blazing wagon — a SR 12-ton open goods — only two small fragments were ever found, the rest ceased to exist. In its place had appeared a crater of 66ft diameter and 15ft depth which completely obliterated 120ft of the passing loop. All Soham's station buildings were largely destroyed and the goods shed, 130 yards away, was heavily damaged. To the east of the railway, the little market town suffered badly from the blast — 15 houses were wrecked; 36 more rendered uninhabitable and 700 other buildings received damage of one sort or another.

Severe though the damage was, only 2 people were killed and 5 seriously injured. The prompt and courageous action of the engine crew in isolating the burning wagon had ensured that only *2½ per cent* of the explosives on the train had detonated. Gimbert and Nightall both received the George Cross: probably the only time both members of an engine's crew have been so honoured.

Due largely to the efforts of 100 US Engineer Troops, the line through Soham was in use again after only 18½ hours — a quite extraordinary feat. After meticulous investigation, the inspecting officer concluded that the fire had been started by a spark from the engine igniting some dry material in the wagon.

*Photos: H. C. Casserley*

## TOO FAST ON THE LMS

Permanent way and engineering work, essential to the safe running of the railways, can also provide their own hazards.

In September 1945, engineering work in Watford tunnel necessitated a diversion for up expresses on the LMS Euston-Crewe main line. At Bourne End they were crossed from the up fast to the up slow line, at a crossover protected by a colour-light distant signal which automatically displayed when the points were set for the crossing. This was backed up by an outer home semaphore and a pair of inner home semaphores, but all these were passed at danger by the driver of the 8.20 pm Perth-Euston sleeping car express. In the early hours of the 30th, at the regulator of Royal Scot 4-6-0 No.6157, he entered the 20 mph restricted crossover at 50 mph, effectively derailing his locomotive and six coaches of his train. In the wreckage beneath the 9 foot embankment he, his fireman, and 36 passengers died.

## REAR END COLLISION

Wooden stock invariably suffered badly when in collision with a steam locomotive, as shown in this incident on the local down line near South Bermondsey, SR, on 21st January 1947. An empty steam train from London Bridge to New Cross Gate, headed by 13 Class 4-4-2T No.2028 running bunker first, ran into the rear of the 10.06 am London Bridge-Crystal Palace electric train in fog. Other accidents have occurred in the vicinity, one of the most recent, in September 1975, writing off diesel No.33041. *Photo: BBC Hulton Picture Library*

## THE DANGEROUS CROSSOVER : 2

Also the scene of more than one accident is Goswick, LNER, where three major derailments have occurred on the same crossover.

On 26th October 1947, A3 Pacific No.60066 *Merry Hampton* and its train, diverted onto the slow line, entered the crossover too fast and were derailed at exactly the same spot as NER No.2005 in 1907 (qv). Again, the driver had missed the signals controlling the crossover and the inspecting officer suggested that his attention had been distracted by an unauthorised passenger on the footplate, a naval friend. *Photo: K. Hoole collection*

## SUN BUCKLES RAILS

Midsummer sun, as every schoolboy knows, can expand steel rails and buckle them. This happened on the LNER between York and Darlington on 5th June 1950. The up 'Flying Scotsman' was travelling at speed near Tollerton when the guard felt a severe jolt. By the time he had stopped his train he could see nothing amiss and, having reported the incident to a platelayer who was passing on a bicycle, he restarted the train. The platelayer cycled on alongside the track and was soon confronted by the sight pictured here: buckled rails and A1 Pacific No.60153 *Flamboyant* and its train off the road.

*Photo: K. Hoole collection*

# AUSTERITY RUNS AMOK

Some of the escapades of unmanned engines which have run amok have passed into railway legend. Sharp, Roberts No.79, for example, which was left unattended in forward gear at Petworth Shed in 1859 and subsequently ran for 17½ miles before being stopped by a passing cleaner: or GWR No.1032 which ran for nine miles in 1871 demolishing *seventeen* sets of level crossing gates.

The WD 2-8-0 shown here, No.77195, was left to its own devices at Neville Hill Shed, Leeds, on 17th September 1950 and ran wrong line through Marsh Lane cutting, through Marsh Lane goods yard and through the boundary wall into Marsh Lane itself.

No.77195 was of interest in having been built with armour plating following Luftwaffe attacks on trains. In this form it was tested at Longmoor but its heavy axle loading offset all the normal benefits of the Austerity 2-8-0 and it reverted to normal before its overseas service in Belgium. It was eventually bought by BR and, as 90172, survived until 1967.

*Photo: K. Hoole collection*

**HATFIELD 1954**

# INTO THE PIT

In 1954 the turntable at Hatfield MPD was removed as it was not required by the tank engines allocated there. On 24th May in that year, N2 No.69638 ran into the pit before it could be filled in: the result of mismanagement by the driver who was moving the engine on the nearby ashpit and failed to stop in time.

*Photo: P. N. Townend*

## TRAP POINTS TROUBLE

January 1955, and the result of a common problem — an engine running through trap points and fouling a crossover. The location was at the exit from Eastleigh MPD, SR, and work went on all night in heavy rain and high wind to clear the obstruction: a reminder that accident repairs always take precedence over all other activities on the railway.
*Photo: C. P. Boocock*

## DRIVER ERROR AT BOURNEMOUTH

Entering Bournemouth Central from Weymouth, the driver of H15 No.30485 found his way barred by N15 No.30783 which had moved after its driver had misread signals. The picture, taken next day (23rd January 1955), shows No.30485 still on its side blocking the exit from the MPD, while No. 30783 has been righted and shunted aside. The former engine was subsequently condemned: the latter needed a new offside half frame and cylinder.     *Photo: C. P. Boocock*

## NEWCASTLE 1955

## CROSSOVER COMPETITION

The drivers of V2 No.60968 and 2-6-4T No.42073, due to misreading of signals, competed for diamond crossovers at the east end of Newcastle Central station on 19th April 1955 and were both derailed.     *Photo: K. Hoole collection*

## FILEY 1956

## NO BRAKES ON STOCK TRAIN

On 25th August 1956, a long empty stock train, headed by K3 No.61846, was approaching Filey Holiday Camp station down the 6¾ mile gradient, when the driver discovered that he only had the engine's brakes to stop the 429 ton train. The brake pipes had not been coupled at Bridlington. No. 61846 hit the buffer stops at the end of platform 3 at about 25 mph, wrecked its bogie and pushed a five-ton block of concrete twenty yards.     *Photo: K. Hoole*

The accident at Hitchin South (*see overleaf*).

## HITCHIN SOUTH 1958

# TRIPLE COLLISION IN FOG

In the early morning hours of 19th November 1958, a triple collision occurred in fog at Hitchin South, ER. Just before 4.30 am, the driver of 9F No.92187, in charge of a down freight, ran past several signals at caution and danger and collided with the rear of a similar train. Soon afterwards, an up freight hauled by V2 No.60885, passing on the up fast line, ran into the wreckage. The wagons of this train knocked over LI No.67785 which was standing on the up slow line. Despite the apparent chaos — which blocked all four running lines — the locomotives were not badly damaged: No.67785 needed a new cylinder casting, No.60885's pony truck was torn off and No.92187's frames were slightly bent. 34 wagons were badly damaged or derailed.

*Photos: News Chronicle, courtesy P. N. Townend*

## ENGINE RAMS SIGNAL BOX

On 20th July 1959, the driver of Jubilee No.45730 *Ocean* was backing down from St Pancras station to the MPD at Kentish Town when he missed a signal at danger. To protect the main line, the points had been set into a short dead end spur, with the result shown here. Handsignalling was in force into and out of St Pancras for several days until the signal box could be repaired.

*Photo: P. N. Townend*

## BULLEIDS IN TROUBLE

SR Pacifics off the road. Above, 34020 *Seaton* nestles in the platform end at St Denys after its driver had misread signals and taken the 6.30 pm Weymouth-Waterloo off the loop and into the sand drag. Photographed on the next day: 31st October 1959.

Below: 34045 *Ottery St Mary* being disentangled from the buffer stops beyond the down platform at Bournemouth Central after running through the trap points at the end of the loop, 2nd September 1961.                         *Photos: C. P. Boocock*

## DEATH OF AN IVATT    *(Right)*

Adolphus Street goods yard in Bradford was the scene of a spectacular mishap on 15th November 1964. Ivatt mogul No.43072 lost control of its train and, as its driver and fireman jumped for their lives, crashed through the buffer stops and the retaining wall to land in Dryden Street. This was in the twilight years of steam traction and No. 43072, with its tender lying on top of it and facing the other way, was not thought to be worth saving. It was sold to a local scrap merchant and ignominiously cut up on the spot.

*Photos: K. Hoole collection*

# IRRESISTIBLE FORCE, IMMOVABLE OBJECT

One of the requirements of the Regulation of Railways Act of 1845 was the provision of gated crossings, worked by railway staff, at all public level crossings. This was to prove a remarkably safe system, no accident involving heavy casualties having ever occurred on a manned level crossing on any British railway. By the 1950's, however, changing conditions were making the manned crossing expensive, cumbersome and slow.. Continental-style automatic half-barrier crossings (AHB's) had been approved in 1957 by BR and the MoT and by the late 1960's they were in widespread use through-out the rapidly modernising British Rail system. Their suitability and the planning and regulations governing their installation and use were to be severely tested as the result of the events on the LMR's electrified Colwich-Manchester main line near the village of Hixon on 6th January 1968.

In the early afternoon of that Saturday, a 42-ton road transporter carrying a huge 120-ton transformer was approaching Hixon crossing, which was situated on a quiet country road and had been converted to AHB some nine months previously. The twin tractors were crewed by five men and escort was provided by two police constables in a patrol car. The special traffic movement had been authorised by the MoT, but the seven men on the spot were almost entirely ignorant of the procedures for taking such a

load across one of the new style crossings.

Proceeding at 4 mph, the massive transporter reached the crossing and there halved its speed to negotiate the uneven surface and low overhead wires. Soon it straddled the tracks and at this point, in a moment of drama rarely equalled in British railway history, the crossing bells began to ring, the lights to flash, and the barriers dropped — one of them falling onto the transformer itself. The wretched individuals at the crossing did not have long to wait.

Almost immediately, electric locomotive No.E3009 appeared around the curve. She was travelling, with the effortless ease of her class, at near her maximum and hauling the 500-ton Manchester-Euston express with some 300 passengers aboard.

Although its driver made an emergency brake application, the engine hit the transformer at about 75 mph and, in the appalling impact, *sheared* the massive transporter and was horribly demolished, along with the first three coaches of its train. The three enginemen died instantly, but due entirely to the strength and stability of modern coaching stock only 8 passengers were killed and 45 injured.

Because of the complex issues arising from it, and the great public outcry, the Hixon disaster was the first railway accident since 1879 to be the subject of a full public enquiry as opposed to an investigation by the Railway Inspectorate. The immediate cause of the accident was the transporter driver's failure to telephone the signalman for permission to cross with an abnormal load, as he was required to do by a roadside notice, but both he and the escorting policemen were ignorant of this regulation. These men were, however, seen by the enquiry as the hapless victims of a widespread failure of planning and communication at all levels; concerning the Hixon incident in particular and the installation and operation of AHB's generally.

AHB's, concluded the enquiry, *were* a useful innovation, but only subject to certain changes and improvements — which were implemented.

Today at Hixon the barriers are still there, but the warning notices are larger and more emphatically worded; there are special lay-bys and telephones for drivers of abnormal loads and, at the nearby electrical depot, transformers similar to the one involved in the disaster stand on low loaders ready for transportation.

*Photos: Stafford/Stone Newsletter*

BARTLOW 1968

## PHONEY WAR

Something of a mystery picture at first glance, this shows an incident in marked contrast to the drama at Hixon. This is a railway 'accident' staged in November 1968 for the cameras, as part of the film 'The Virgin Soldiers' and intended to represent an incident in darkest Malaya. The location is in fact in darkest Cambridgeshire, on the old Great Eastern branch from Shelford to Long Melford. The engine is a condemned Black 5, suitably disguised as a Malayan tank engine. Other railway sequences for the film were shot in Malaya itself.

*Photo: Lens of Sutton*

## WARNING SIGNS UNLIT

At 11.30 pm on 5th June 1975 the electrically hauled sleeping car express left Euston for Glasgow. Because of engine failure, it was running an hour late by the time it reached Nuneaton, where a 20 mph speed restriction was in force due to major permanent way work. The gas-lit speed restriction warning sign 1¼ miles out, had failed and was not illuminated and the driver of locomotive No.86 242 did not reduce speed until he was upon the second warning sign — itself only partially lit — at the actual commencement of the restricted section. Here he made a full emergency brake application but it was far too late. At approaching 70 mph the express derailed in Nuneaton station, killing 6 and injuring 38.

*Photo: Birmingham Post & Mail*

## LUNAN BAY 1975

### FATAL PHONE CALL

An unusual rear end collision occurred between Montrose and Arbroath, Scottish Region, on 26th October 1975. Due to locomotive failure, the 10.15 Aberdeen-King's Cross express came to a stand at Lunan Bay, where the guard telephoned for an assisting engine. Although familiar with the route, he inadvertently gave the location of his train as Lethan Grange — which lay some five miles further south. Thus, the crew of hurrying relief engine No.40 111 were surprised to see the express's guard at Lunan Bay and to hear, too late, the sound of the detonators he had placed exploding under their wheels. Seconds later their engine rammed the rear of the stranded express at about 25 mph, killing one person and injuring 42.

*Photo: D. C. Thompson & Co. Ltd*

## JUST ROUTINE

The latest in motive power in trouble at Bristol on 11th September 1977. HST power car No.253 005 had derailed itself while working empty stock and the brakedown crew are performing a routine recovery job. On such occasions, speed is essential for even minor incidents can lead to wholesale disruption of traffic.

*Photo: Les Bertram*

## THE SHAPE OF THINGS TO COME?

Vandalism has never been a complete stranger to the railways, but in recent years the number of reported incidents has increased alarmingly. The scene here shows the Aberdeen-King's Cross sleeper at Prestonpans, south of Edinburgh, on 22nd May 1980. A youth had placed a length of rail across the track. Although it was travelling at high speed when derailed, the strength and stability of modern coaching stock was again demonstrated and there were no serious injuries. An outbreak of 'copy-cat' vandalism was soon after reported on the Midland main line. Malicious damage promises to be one of BR's most pressing problems in the years ahead and it remains to be seen how effective their efforts to combat this new threat to the safe passage of trains will be.

*Photo: C. P. Boocock*

# HEAD-ON COLLISION

This photograph provides sombre evidence that the crew of a modern locomotive are ill-protected in the event of a head-on collision, and also that new technology can never completely guarantee the safe passage of trains. The Brush 47 hauling the

21.50 York-Manchester mail was at a stand at Farnley Junction, Leeds, on 5th September 1977 when it was hit by the 20.40 Liverpool-Hull dmu. Due to faulty wiring in a lineside electrical cabinet the junction's signals and points had operated incorrectly, with the result that both trains were directed onto the same running line. The two drivers died and 15 people were injured.

*Photo: Yorkshire Post*